SEX POSITIONS
FOR BEGINNERS

How-To Guide For Men And Women To Deep Into The
Most Exciting Sex Positions And Dirty Sexy Games That
Will Make Desire Explode, Enjoying Sex More Than Ever
Before

Melany Evans

Table of Contents

INTRODUCTION

Tantric sex urges individuals to become acquainted with their own bodies and become on top of them. By understanding the craving of one's own body, one can consolidate this during sex with an accomplice. This may prompt more prominent sexual satisfaction and more serious climaxes.

To comprehend what one's body needs, it tends to be valuable to take part in tantric confidence or masturbation.

If an individual finds that they have passionate squares around self-contact, they ought to be interested and delicate with themselves as they investigate what is keeping them from becoming acquainted with their own body all the more personally.

In opposition to standard discernment, the Kama Sutra isn't just a sex manual jam-pressed with unpredictable and unusual positions to flavor up your adoration life. Or maybe it's a thick, consecrated content that presents an investigation of want, closeness and living through a feeling of unhinged interest and freedom.

There are prompts about different styles of kissing, grasping, and contacting.

"It's tied in with developing into your body and making new disclosures about yourself and your commitment with your accomplice," says Keeley Rankin, MA, sex advisor, and relationship mentor.

So while sexual stances are just a small amount of what the antiquated content includes, fortunately we diverted astuteness from the sexperts and gathered together a couple of its most stimulating takeaways.

Ahead are answers to generally posed inquiries about the Kama Sutra, just as nine positions for you and your accomplice to try different things with together—ones sure to twist your adaptability and raise your sexual association with new (ahem) statures...

Before you get into position, remember a couple of things...

In spite of the fact that you might be enticed to surge off to the room, Dr. David Yarian, Ph.D., authorized analyst and certified sex advisor, recommends that you first abandon your desires and decisions... basically welcome an environment of play.

Because while you and your accomplice might be eager to draw motivation from the Kama Sutra's wellspring of sexual stances, you shouldn't turn out to be so overwhelmed by performing them "effectively" that you miss the excellence of the excursion, which is an audacious delight. "I urge my customers to investigate exotic touch, figuring out how to 'taste' or 'peruse' one another. The thought is to increase affectability to joy, regardless of whether giving or accepting," says Dr. Yarian.

The more an individual thinks about their body and joy zones, the more probable they are to have a delightful sexual encounter.

If somebody doesn't wish to participate in masturbation and has an accomplice, be that as it may, they may feel more great finding out about their own body through banded together sex.

Knowing One's Accomplice's Body

Tantric sex is tied in with regarding one's body and the body of one's accomplice. By setting aside some effort to become acquainted with one's own body just as that of one's accomplice, it can help make the experience satisfying for the two individuals.

An individual may consider giving their accomplice a moderate, full-body back rub to find out about their body and help stir their sexual energy. This may likewise enable an individual to become in line with their accomplice's needs and wants.

Similar to the case with any sexual activity, if anytime an individual or their accomplice gets awkward, the movement should stop.

The Most Effective Method to Plan

There are a couple of things an individual or couple can never really plan for tantric sex. For instance, they can:

Put aside time: Tantric sex is tied in with moving gradually and being at the time. Sometimes, it can be most recent an hour or more. Therefore, make certain to put aside some an ideal opportunity to completely connect with and appreciate the experience.

Set up the brain: Focusing on the second can be difficult if an individual is encountering pressure or has numerous things at the forefront of their thoughts. Contemplating or extending before tantric sex may help accomplish an unmistakable attitude.

Locate a decent spot: Environment has a critical part in tantric sex. In a perfect world, it will happen in a loosening upsetting with an agreeable temperature. An individual might need to diminish the lights, light a scented flame, or put on loosening up music.

Building the Second with an Accomplice

To fabricate the second with an accomplice, individuals can attempt the accompanying tips:

Receive a hand-on-heart position: To increase a profound association, couples ought to sit with folded legs and face one another. The two accomplices should put their correct hand on the other's heart, with the left hand on their partner's. Feel the association and attempt to synchronize relaxing.

Try not to go direct: Normally, sexual exercises may follow a content of foreplay, intercourse, and climax. Nonetheless, tantric sex is tied in with testing, so it is ideal to remain open to what particularly feels great at the time.

Visually connect: Making eye to eye connection may help extend the association and increase closeness.

Take things moderate: Tantric sex is reflective and about investigating sensations at the time. This cycle should be a moderate and agreeable excursion for the two accomplices.

Breathing Procedure

Breathing is a necessary piece of tantric sex. This is halfway because tantric sex rotates around contemplation.

During tantric sex, an individual should zero in on breathing profoundly through the stomach. To accomplish this, they should take a full breath through the nose for five tallies. They should feel their stomach expand. They should then breathe out through the mouth for five checks.

When participating in tantric sex with an accomplice, synchronizing the breath may build association and closeness.

Another breathing procedure individuals can attempt is Kapalbhati. Kapalbhati drags out discharge in guys. When a male feels that they are going to discharge, they ought to strongly breathe out through the mouth, then take part in a programmed breathe in through the mouth.

CHAPTER 1. TANTRIC MASSAGE

Tantric back rub is a magnificent method to interface with your accomplice, yet there's something else entirely to it than just playing out a sexual back rub.

With its profoundly otherworldly roots, tantra includes the equilibrium and entwining of energy among you and your accomplice, and rehearsing tantric back rub can therefore assist with strengthening your bond and lead to a more profound comprehension between you both.

Peruse on to study the advantages of tantric back rub and how to perform one.

What is Tantric Back Rub?

Anyway, it's in excess of a sensual back rub – yet how, precisely?

'With establishes situated in old treatment yet with an advanced wind, tantric back rub empowers you to associate with your accomplice in a more otherworldly and cognizant manner, making unwinding and quietness a definitive objective,' clarifies Nadia Deen, prime supporter of The Intimology. 'It's not "one size fits all" – all things being equal, it's tied in with being available at the time, and tolerating ourselves and each other without judgment.

Connecting all your chakras and utilizing the transaction of energy, tantric back rub can be a profoundly fulfilling experience for the two players.'

Sex and closeness mentor, Camilla Constance, concurs that being available and nonjudgemental is vital to empower the recipient to drop into profound unwinding.

'A tantric back rub is a full-body knead that stirs sexual energy in the beneficiary and afterward deliberately moves that energy around the body,' she clarifies. 'It's a beautiful method to encounter the tantric way to deal with sex, where it isn't about the objective or result, yet about each snapshot of sensation and joy in transit.

Because of the degree of unwinding that the recipient can fall into, as sexual energy fabricates, it isn't constrained out of the body in a concise peak, however, it can move around the body, developing into mind-blowing, full-bodied climaxes.

When cognizant breathing is added, the degree of energy increments, and the experience is additionally elevated.

A tantric back rub is a full-body knead that stirs sexual energy in the collector.

Tantric back Rub Benefits

Just as offering a protected space to investigate each other without weight or judgment, tantric back rub has other ground-breaking benefits. 'Aside from finding another and more profound closeness with your partner(s), there are numerous other medical advantages,' uncovers Deen. She says these include:

- Improving your sexual endurance

- Improving the nature of your climaxes

- Assisting with facilitating torment

- Giving pressure help

- Improving rest

- A decent advance towards recuperating passionate blockages

- Aiding profound arousing

The Recuperating Intensity of Tantra

One of the most beautiful advantages of tantric back rub and tantric sex is its capacity to assist somebody with recuperating from – and rise above – past injury. 'Tantra isn't about proliferation,' says Constance. 'All things being equal, tantra offers a totally new (to us) idea of the reason for sex.

To our exceptionally molded personalities, we can scarcely envision heterosexual sex without infiltration, because what is the purpose of sex if this demonstration doesn't occur? Tantra would reply – consistently – the fact of the matter is joy. This completely exposes!

The one who has endured a vaginal injury, through possibly a difficult birth or sexual attack; the man with erectile brokenness or untimely discharge, or even a little penis, is at this point don't sexually "broken" and needing fixing with lubes, pills, or treatment. They are beautiful spirits with bodies that can encounter joy in heap ways. Tantra is the specialty of learning new courses to sexual delight.

'Tantra instructs us that we don't have to infiltrate a vagina with a penis to encounter fantastic sexual delight and stunning climaxes. Tantra is the craft of learning new courses to sexual delight, so as to support and continue upbeat, solid lives and relationships.'

Tantric Back Rub Arrangement

Before the back rub starts, invest a little energy guaranteeing the back rub climate is helpful for unwinding. It merits thinking about the accompanying:

Climate

Both Deen and Constance state that making a beautifully quiet and serene space is vital to a tantric back rub.

'Your environmental factors are similarly as significant as the back rub itself, so invest some energy arranging your current circumstance,' says Deen. 'Think about the temperature, look, sound, and feel of the room.'

Your environmental factors are similarly as significant as the back rub itself.

Constance concurs that connecting all the faculties is significant.

'The more hallowed space, the more beautiful the back rub will be,' she uncovers. 'Tantra instructs us to get to sex – and life – with the entirety of our faculties, so what we see, smell, taste, and hear around us during the back rub will totally effect on the experience.

'Put on crisp sheet material if you are giving the back rub on your bed, turn down the lights, light candles, play beautiful music, sprinkle unadulterated basic oils on the bed or have some in a diffuser to occupy the space with beautiful fragrance.'

Oil

When it comes to tantric back rub, oil is something of a prerequisite, as per Constance.

'A beautiful oil is basic for making this experience amazingly sexy,' she says. 'I would venture to such an extreme as to train you not to endeavor a tantric back rub without oil. I'm in favor of coconut oil, yet others depend on olive oil. Any 100% normal oil extricated from plants is acceptable.'

Time

Similarly as with all parts of tantra, tantric back rub can't be surged.

'Ensure you have the opportunity to completely enjoy your accomplice's pleasure,' says Deen. 'Mood killer your telephone and your email notifications.

If you live with others, ensure you won't be upset by their essence or commotion.

It's fundamental that you can feel totally calm in your environmental factors. There's nothing more vibe executing than hurrying.'

Mentality

At long last, ensure you are in the perfect spot intellectually, profoundly, and inwardly.

'To give this kind of back rub, it's imperative that you are in the correct perspective heretofore,' clarifies Deen. 'To evade transaction of undesirable energy, being quiet and focused is vital, so put in no time flat in advance in a peaceful space clearing your musings and focusing on your own breathing, and urge your accomplice to do likewise.'

Instructions to play out a tantric back rub

When the state of mind is set, presently it's an ideal opportunity to get familiar with the craft of tantric back rub itself. Here's our bit by bit manage...

Unwind

Constance reminds that the main viewpoint is to unwind completely into the experience.

'It's simple when you're giving a back rub to stress, "Am I doing this right? Have I got the correct procedure?"' she says. 'Unwind! I can't pressure how significant it is when you give a back rub that you unwind and appreciate the body you are kneading.'

Back of the body

Constance says to begin the rear of their body.

'The individual accepting the back rub lies face down on the bed, and the provider goes through between 20 minutes and thirty minutes rubbing the rear of their body, utilizing a lot of oil,' she says. 'Kneading the rear of somebody's body is your training zone!

Set aside the effort to develop your certainty, affectability, and most importantly, your ability to give. Become truly aware of the body underneath your palms and fingertips, see how it responds to different kinds of touch and different weights.

Different individuals like their touch in different manners, and what they appreciate will change as their sexual energy changes. It's your employment as the provider to peruse the signs from the getting body and get the master on them.'

Become truly aware of the body underneath your palms and fingertips, see how it responds to different kinds of touch and weights.

Front of the body

'The second phase of the back rub is moving to the front of the body,' Constance says. 'At this point, the collector ought to be profoundly loose, so request that they turn throughout and invest energy rubbing every last bit of the front of their body.

For the present, do close to tenderly prod the lingam [penis] or yoni [vulva and vagina] by brushing over them as you take care of the remainder of the body.

'Back rub the legs, feet, between the toes, hands, each finger and arms, and pay specific praise to the bosoms and midsection. These are delicate, weak regions within each one of us, and it's staggeringly recuperating to have them kneaded tenderly and with affection.'

The Lingam/Yoni Rub

Constance says it's imperative to go through at any rate 20 minutes rubbing the front of your accomplice's body prior to proceeding onward to the lingam or yoni rub.

'It's critical to be truly certain that there is no normal or right result from a lingam or yoni knead,' she reminds. 'This back rub is a takeoff from desires, recollect? It's tied in with giving the recipient the reality to interface with sensation and joy in their body in totally new ways.

Because we're so adapted to react to sexual energy in a restricted, objective situated way, it's on the part of the provider to back the entire cycle off. Give the energy time to develop, notice how it fabricates and monitor it. This requires some serious energy and practice, and is the reason giving a wonderful tantric back rub is a workmanship.'

Step-by-Step Instructions to Play Out a Lingam Knead

'If you are rubbing a lingam, watch out for the speed of their excitement,' says Constance. 'If it's getting too hot too early, slow things directly down.

Try not to fear loss of an erection – it doesn't make a difference, you can, without much of a stretch, develop it once more. Try not to fear them discharging "too early" – they can really keep on encountering joy and energy post-discharge, so proceed with the back rub, and if the lingam is excessively delicate, move the back rub back to the remainder of the body. Try not to fear the collector not discharging, permit them (and you) to encounter sexual energy in new ways.

'All things being equal, gotten a specialist in all the different manners to contact and give joy. A lingam rub isn't a hand work! Find out about the different delight spots on the lingam and how they react to different kinds of touch.

There are five key zones to comprehend and joy: the organs, the frenulum (if it hasn't been taken out), the pole, the balls, and the perineum.'

Costance says that this sort of moderate, waiting back rub can be extraordinarily mending.

'What you have to comprehend when you give a lingam knead is how much dread this lingam has encountered; how much weight it has been under to "perform,"' says Constance. 'When you can gift this total love and acknowledgment to a lingam, you venture into an unheard of level of intensity.'

The most Effective Method to Play Out a Yoni Knead

Similarly as with the mending intensity of the lingam knead, the equivalent is valid for a yoni rub – actually, significantly more so.

'If you're kneading a yoni, it's critical to comprehend the degree of disgrace, dread, disengage, injury, and trouble experienced in this ideal gem,' says Constance. 'You are in a position to add to the injury or recuperate it. Giving a yoni rub is one of the most mending gifts a sweetheart can give. What's more, because it can possibly be so stunning, it likewise can possibly do extraordinary mischief.

Because of this, you totally should respect and regard the yoni consistently. You move at your accomplice's movement and go where they need you to go.

To realize where that is, you gotten a specialist on this yoni, you watch your accomplice change as excitement levels change, you watch out for the remainder of the body, and you tune in to uplifting statements and direction originating from your accomplice, who must feel no weight from you to act in any capacity.

'The yoni rub is an occasion to give the outside of the yoni a ton of time and consideration. Utilizing loads of oil, stroke, bother, and delight the vulva: the external and internal lips, the fourchette, the perineum, the launch of the vagina, the clitoral bud and clitoral roots.

'Simply following a decent 15 minutes of pleasuring the vulva, would you be able to put a finger at the launch of the vagina and check whether you are invited inside. It's in every case, great practice to ask for authorization.

If the appropriate response is no, invest more energy on the vulva and expand the strokes around the whole body, moving the sensation and joy to every last trace of the body.

'If your accomplice might want you to enter with your fingers, do so gradually. Move in each centimeter in turn and in round developments, as though you are circumventing the focuses on the clock, and apply delicate strain to the dividers of the vagina.

You are not fingering her – the thought isn't to consistently pushed your finger all through the vagina. You are kneading the dividers of the vagina, then her G-spot, and afterward her cervix, gradually, intentionally and with massive love.'

Finishing the Back Rub

If tantric back rub doesn't come full circle with climax, how would you realize when to stop?

'When and how to end the back rub is trying for those of us adapted into the Western model of sex,' says Constance. 'Finishing the back rub because the recipient has peaked totally nullifies the point of the back rub, so

I recommend you just end the back rub following 90 minutes, and after no under 30 minutes of offering joy to the lingam or yoni, whatever occurs.

'I additionally recommend the back rub isn't utilized as an antecedent for penetrative sex. Clearly it's significant not to be too unbending about this, because penetrative sex in the energy made by a tantric back rub is unbelievable.

Notwithstanding, it transforms the back rub into simple foreplay, which can lessen its capacity.'

CHAPTER 2. SEXUAL ENERGY

B ecause it's an imperative point for anybody inspired by accomplishment, self-advancement, mental development, and profound development.

Sexual change is likewise another of those terribly misjudged points. How about we change that at this moment.

Endurance can mean numerous things, however, when it comes to sex, it often alludes to how long you can get rearward in bed.

For guys, the normal time between the sheets is somewhere in the range of two to five minutes. For females, it's somewhat more: around 20 minutes prior to arriving at the enormous O.

If you're unsatisfied with how rapidly you carry out the thing, there are various things you can attempt to support your endurance and improve your general sexual exhibition.

Peruse on to find out additional.

Masturbation Can Help Develop Perseverance

Masturbation can assist you with enduring longer in bed by delivering up developed sexual pressure.

If you have a penis, you may think that its accommodating to:

- Change it up by utilizing your non-prevailing hand.

- Spin and push your hips to expand power.

- Attempt different strokes to flavor up your independent fun.

- Utilize one hand to keep an eye on your penis and the other to play with your balls.

- Animate your prostate for a more profound climax.

If you have a vagina, you may think that it's supportive to:

- Consolidate a blend of clitoral, vaginal, and butt-centric play.

- Add some lube to build your pleasure.

- Turn up the warmth by investigating your erogenous zones — like your neck, areolas, or thighs.

- Present a sex toy — or two — to increase the joy.

- Think about watching, tuning in, or perusing some erotica or sexual entertainment. Shop for ointment.

Exercise Can Help Develop Quality

If you need to expand your endurance, you'll have to develop your quality. A more grounded body can bear more, permitting you to last more between the sheets.

Biceps

More grounded biceps implies you can deal with more weight when lifting, pulling, throwing, and tossing.

Activities to attempt include:

- bicep twists

- jawline ups

- twisted around column

Rear Arm Muscles

Solid rear arm muscles make pushing simpler, however, they likewise develop the intensity of your chest area.

Activities to attempt include:

- seat press

- rear arm muscles augmentation

- rear arm muscles pull-down or push-down

Pectoral

You utilize your pectoral muscles for all that you do — from making a way for lifting a glass. When you have more grounded pecs, you have a more grounded body generally.

Activities to attempt include:

- seat press

- chest plunges

- push-ups

Stomach

When you have solid abs, you have an all the more remarkable center. Also, when you have a solid center, you're more adjusted and feel less back torment.

Activities to attempt include:

- sit-ups

- boards

- high knees

Lower Back

A solid lower back balances out and bolsters your spine, just as reinforces your center.

Activities to attempt include:

- spans

- lying parallel leg raise

- superman augmentation

Pelvic Floor

Your pelvic floor controls your privates, which implies if you need to expand your sexual endurance, you have to construct solid — and adaptable — pelvic floor muscles.

Activities to attempt include:

- Kegels

- squats

- spans

Glutes

Frail glutes can lose your adjustment and stiffen your hips, which will influence your presentation in bed.

Activities to attempt include:

- squats

- weighted rushes

- hip expansion

Quads and Hamstrings

Your quad and hamstrings power your hips and knees, which implies the more grounded those muscles are, the quicker and longer you can go.

Activities to attempt include:

- leg press

- rushes

- venture up

Exercise Can Likewise Improve Adaptability

When your muscles are free and adaptable, you have a more full scope of movement, which implies you can accomplish more — much more — in bed.

Standing hamstring stretch (for the neck, back, glutes, hamstrings, and calves):

- Remain with your feet hip-width separated, knees twisted marginally, and arms resting by your sides.

- Breathe out as you twist forward at the hips.

- Lower your head toward the floor, loosening up your head, neck, and shoulders.

- Fold your arms over your legs, holding the posture for at any rate 45 seconds.

- Then, twist your knees and move up.

Leaning back bound point present (for internal thigh, hips, and crotch):

- While lying on your back, bring the bottoms of your feet together, permitting your knees to open up and draw nearer to the floor.

- Keep your arms at your sides, palms looking down on the ground.

- Hold the posture for at any rate 30 seconds.

Lurch with spinal bend (for hip flexors, quads, and back):

- Get into a forward lurch position beginning with your left foot.

- Spot your correct hand on the floor.

- Curve your chest area to one side, broadening your left arm toward the roof.

- Hold this posture for in any event 30 seconds, and afterward, rehash on the correct side.

Rear arm muscles stretch (for the neck, shoulders, back, and rear arm muscles):

- Broaden your arms overhead.

- Twist your correct elbow, and arrive at your correct hand so that it's contacting the top center of your back.

- Utilize your left hand to snatch just underneath your correct elbow, and pull your correct elbow down delicately.

- Hold for around 15 to 30 seconds, then rehash with the left arm.

Exercise to consistent your breath and strengthen your tongue

Notwithstanding loosening up your psyche, controlling your breath permits your body to give your muscles more oxygen-rich blood.

This can prompt a lower pulse and may bring about a superior generally execution.

Strengthening your tongue can likewise help improve your breathing, just as increment your endurance for oral sex.

For a solid tongue, attempt these activities:

- Tongue pull-back. Stick your tongue out straight, then draw it back in your mouth as far as possible. Hold this position for 2 seconds. Rehash multiple times.

- Tongue push-ups. Push the lower part of the tip of your tongue as hard as possible into the front of the top of your mouth, directly behind your teeth. Rehash 5 to multiple times.

Key Supplements for Generally Execution

Need to improve your exhibition in bed? Then ensure you're getting enough of these key supplements.

For Everybody

Capsaicin: Capsaicin is found in most hot peppers, so no big surprise it helps supports your perseverance. It likewise accelerates recuperation, which implies you can go again in the blink of an eye.

Capsaicin-rich nourishments include:

- stew peppers

- sweet peppers

- ginger root

Potassium: One of the body's most significant electrolytes, potassium keeps your muscles, and cells hydrated, guides in recuperation, and lifts your digestion — which is all significant if you need to keep up your endurance.

Potassium-rich nourishments include:

- banana

- melon

- spinach

- broccoli

- white potato

- tomatoes

- carrot

- low-fat milk or yogurt

- quinoa

Complex carbs: Simple carbs found in pasta and bread can murder your endurance rapidly. In any case, complex carbs do the specific inverse: They help give your body an enduring jolt of energy.

Nourishments with complex carbs include:

- cereal

- sweet potatoes and yams

- entire wheat bread

- earthy colored rice and wild rice

- quinoa, grain, bulgur, and other entire grains

- corn

- peas and dried beans

Protein: Protein takes longer than carbs to separate, giving your body a more extended, enduring wellspring of energy.

Nourishments pressed with protein include:

- nuts

- tofu

- eggs

- lean red meat, poultry, and fish

- yogurt, cheddar, and milk

B nutrients: B nutrients — particularly B-1 to B-5, and B-12 — direct your sex hormone levels and capacity, which helps give your charisma and execution a lift.

Nourishments plentiful in B nutrients include:

- lean meat, fish, and poultry

- eggs

- nutty spread

- avocado

- fortified and enhanced grains

- milk and dairy items

- verdant green vegetables

Omega-3s: Omega-3s are basic unsaturated fats that help balance your sex hormones, giving your drive and endurance a pleasant lift.

Nourishments pressed with omega-3s include:

- flaxseed, chia seeds, and hemp

- kale and spinach

- pecans

- mussels

- fish and other slick fish

Specifically for Guys

L-citrulline: Research has indicated that L-citruline, a normally happening amino corrosive, can build quality and endurance. It might likewise help you keep up an erection.

Nourishments high in L-citrulline include:

- watermelon

- onions and garlic

- vegetables and nuts

- salmon and red meat

- dull chocolate

L-arginine: The body changes over L-citrulline to L-arginine, another amino corrosive that improves bloodstream and assembles protein.

Nourishments with L-arginine include:

- red meat, fish, and poultry

- soy

- entire grains

- beans

- milk, yogurt, and other dairy items

Nitrates: Nitrates improves how your muscles use oxygen, which can help upgrade your exhibition — inside and outside the room.

Nitrate-rich nourishments include:

- arugula, swiss chard, and other verdant greens

- beets and beet juice

- rhubarb

- carrots

- eggplant

- celery

Magnesium: Magnesium is a fundamental supplement that assumes a vital part in everything from energy to cerebrum work. So when your magnesium levels are low, your endurance is exhausted.

Nourishments high in magnesium include:

- entire wheat

- spinach and other dull verdant greens

- quinoa

- almonds, cashews, and peanuts

- dark beans

- edamame

Specifically for Females

Folic corrosive: Folic corrosive invigorates the turn of events and development of new cells, which assists battle with fatigue and lift endurance.

Nourishments stuffed with folic corrosive include:

- avocado

- lentils

- dried beans, peas, and nuts

- broccoli, spinach, asparagus, and other dull green vegetables

- citrus natural products

Calcium: Calcium keeps bones solid and thick, which is significant for your cells to work appropriately and keep your energy up.

Calcium-rich nourishments include:

- skim milk

- cheddar

- low-fat yogurt

- salmon, sardines, and other fish with eatable bones

Nutrient D: Vitamin D underpins bone wellbeing and invulnerability, lifts your state of mind, and encourages you to keep up a solid weight — all essential parts in expanding your endurance.

Incredible wellsprings of nutrient D include:

- salmon and sardines

- egg yolk

- shrimp

- fortified milk, grain, yogurt, and squeezed orange

Iron: Iron is a vital supplement in keeping up energy and a sound digestion, which, thus, helps construct endurance.

Iron-rich nourishments include:

- red meat, poultry, and fish

- fortified oats

- kale, spinach, and other verdant greens

- lentils and beans

Spices for in General Execution

Need a characteristic method to improve your endurance? Then home grown enhancements might be your answer.

For Everybody

Damiana. This subtropical plant is thought to increment sexual desire and endurance.

Guarana. This Brazilian plant has a high caffeine content that is accepted to help energy and drive.

Maca. This profoundly nutritious Peruvian plant is viewed as a sex drive enhancer.

Specifically for guys

Ginseng. This moderate developing, short plant is accepted to improve indications of erectile dysfunction.

Catuaba. This little tree local to Brazil is viewed as a love potion. It might likewise help treat erectile brokenness.

Lycium. Otherwise called goji berry, this Chinese natural product plant is thought to build testosterone levels and treat erectile brokenness.

Shop for ginseng and catuaba.

Specifically for females

Ginkgo biloba. This Chinese plant concentrate may give your sex drive some oomph, just as lift intellectual prowess and energy.

Ashwagandha. This evergreen bush is accepted to improve drive and endurance by controlling sex hormones.

Shop for ginkgo biloba and ashwagandha.

Different Tips and Deceives

Working out, changing your eating routine, and taking enhancements are largely powerful approaches to expand your perseverance. However, potential outcomes don't stop there. You may likewise think that it's accommodating to:

Breaking point liquor consumption heretofore. Liquor influences everyone differently, except drinking a lot before sex can dull your sensations and make it harder for you to remain excited.

Foreplay is significant. Gradually feed the blazes with a touch of foreplay prior to detonating into the headliner.

Grease. Lube can make sex more pleasant by eliminating the rubbing. Certain lubes, similar to desensitizers, can likewise enable your cavort to last more.

Be available. Try not to surge your sex meeting. All things being equal, be available at the time, appreciating each experience of joy.

Investigate something other than the private parts. If you center around the private parts, you're bound to climax rapidly. All things considered, go slow and investigate the entire to develop want.

Switch back and forth among dynamic and latent jobs. Exchanging between jobs will permit your excitement to go in and out like waves, which will make sex last more.

If you have a penis, snatching at the base may help forestall untimely discharge. Crushing at the base will make you lose a portion of your erection and prevent you from peaking.

Applying a desensitizing cream to the tip can likewise help forestall untimely discharge. A desensitizing cream can help reduce the sensations in the penis to assist you with enduring longer.

When to See a Specialist or Other Medical Services Supplier

It's typical for your endurance to be lazy now and again. Yet, if it's determined or joined by different side effects, it very well may be an indication of a fundamental condition.

Make a meeting with a specialist or other medical services supplier if you:

- feel agony or distress during or after sex

- experience issues discharging or arriving at climax

- can't keep an erection

Your supplier can evaluate your indications and assist you with discovering alleviation. If you don't as of now have an essential consideration specialist, the Healthline FindCare instrument can assist you with finding a doctor in your general vicinity.

What is Sexual Transmutation?

Napoleon Hill's self-improvement exemplary, Think and Grow Rich, is the number of people initially find out about sexual change:

"Sex change is basic and handily clarified. It implies the exchanging of the brain from considerations of actual articulation, to contemplations of some other nature."

Presently, Hill's definition is a decent beginning, however we can go further.

Sexual change is the way toward changing over sexual energy into some other drive, inspiration, or energy of a higher request.

Yet, I'm not catching that's meaning?

What is Sexual Energy?

To clarify this present, how about we take a gander at sexual energy through a representation of the seven chakras.

The chakras are supposed to be seven energy places in the body where each chakra identifies with a specific organ in the endocrine framework.

Sexual energy is essential for your life power. This energy emerges from the first or root chakra and the second or sacral chakra.

The root chakra is related to your conceptive organs, while the sacral chakra identifies with your adrenals.

Every one of the seven chakras associates through a spiraling energy channel that moves up the body (kundalini). What's more, this whole energy framework is filled by the base: the home of sexual energy.

Sexual Energy and Pleasure

The sacral chakra manages delight. In spite of the fact that there are a couple of exemptions, most creatures don't have intercourse for delight. Humans, macaques, orangutans, gorillas, and chimpanzees, in any case, do.

When the sacral chakra is in balance, this drive for sexual delight remains with some restraint. Yet, when something deters and debilitates this sexual energy place, it prompts a wide range of issues like sex addictions, depravities, pornography addictions, and forceful conduct.

Sexual Transmutation: From Pleasure to Willpower

Communicating sexual energy through sex and want disseminates this energy. That is, sexual energy goes in one of two headings: out through the sex organ or up into the higher energy communities.

The reason for sexual change is to take your sexual energy and channel it into a higher energy community.

The chakra over the sacral is the sun oriented plexus chakra, which manages self-discipline.

So if an individual needs resolve, there's a decent possibility that their sexual energy is spilling out by means of unnecessary sex, masturbation, incitement, want, stress, or overthinking.

It's hence the self-improvement writing talks about sexual change. For youngsters specifically, if they can channel their drive for sex and lady into their expert work, they increment their resolution to understand their objectives and accomplish more.

There's significantly more to sexual change past accomplishment. Yet, before we continue, we should plot how accomplishment driven sexual change functions.

Step-by-step instructions to Use Sexual Energy Transmutation to Manifest Your Desires

Utilizing sexual energy change to accomplish a specific objective or manifest something (or somebody) in your life is a clear cycle.

Stage 1: Clarify What You Need

Decide your objective:

- Record it.

- Make a picture in your brain.

- Carry it alive in your creative mind with sight, sound, and movement.

- Partner positive feelings to the result.

- Remain quiet about the objective.

In opposition to mainstream thinking, both objective examination and my own experience recommend that it's ideal for keeping your longing or objective to yourself as opposed to reporting it to the world.

Stage 2: Channel Your Consideration Toward Your Objective

Frequently, our energy and consideration get divided into numerous bearings, including sexual cravings. To utilize sexual change, you will channel this sexual energy into the picture of your ideal result.

Keep in mind, we lose sexual energy that streams out. So as opposed to communicating this drive, keep up your consideration on the objective you want.

It's hence Napoleon Hill expounded on the significance of having a "passionate longing." Your craving for what you need must be more noteworthy than your drive for joy at the present time.

Associate with why you need it—your motivation for accomplishing it.

Stage 3: Maintain Your Concentration and Show Restraint

With reestablished life, groundbreaking thoughts will probably start to introduce themselves. The universe, as Hill composes, creatures to plot in support of yourself. You'll line up with partners to help you on your journey. Furthermore, force will begin to manufacture.

Stick with this cycle sufficiently long, and relying upon the object of your craving, you'll start to manifest it.

For What Reason Does This Process Work?

Rather than guiding your attention to irregular transient musings and joys, you're directing your life power energy into making something in the actual world.

This change cycle normally happens for the Magician prime example. Over the long run, you'll learn the subtleties of this cycle and refine it dependent on your disposition.

What Are the Limitations of this Form of Sexual Transmutation?

At last, you may detect a more profound calling. Or on the other hand, you may get bored with utilizing your sexual energy along these lines.

Through a profound arousing, you may start to see that your self-image is playing a game. The personality is continually making new longings, not founded on the Spirit's Will, however on begrudge, voracity, outrage, and dread. Accomplishment starts to lose its rush.

Then, there's a shift from outer accomplishment to internal change. You start to see that you can utilize sexual change to change yourself. Then, things get additionally intriguing.

7 Reasons to Pursue Sexual Transmutation

So now how about we rapidly survey a portion of the reasons people might be keen on sexual change and the potential advantages it can create.

1) Improve Your Physical Health

An essential bit of leeway of sexual change is that it can profoundly improve our imperativeness, life span, and generally speaking, actual wellbeing. Likewise, if you experience the ill effects of lower back or knee torment, there's a decent possibility it's identified with your kidneys, and sex change can help.

2) Achieve Material Success

We talked about this above. Higher accomplishment is the most well-known utilization of sex change.

3) Cultivate More Physical Energy

Semen has more than 200 different proteins, nutrients, minerals, and amino acids. It's a money box of supplements that the body and brain need to perform at their best. Sexual action can exhaust your life power while sexual change develops it.

4) Unlock More Creativity

Sexual energy is additionally imaginative energy. Furthermore, the sexual energy we don't use during sex can be diverted into the innovative cycle.

5) Improve Your Sex Life

When we drain our sexual energy, we have a low charisma or sex drive. In men, this often prompts feebleness. Through sexual change and having intercourse with some restraint, one can improve their sex life.

6) Develop Martial and Internal Power

Eastern material craftsmen and qigong specialists utilize sexual change to develop inner force by changing over sexual energy into chi. Numerous expert competitors do as such as well.

7) Achieve Higher Spiritual Development

Maybe the most elevated utilization of sexual change is to utilize it to stir and develop the Spirit inside.

What Blocks Sexual Transmutation?

Sexual change, from a central perspective, is a characteristic cycle. When we're not changing sexual energy into innovative energy and self-control, it implies something is hindering or misleading it.

Buddhists call this confusion extravagance, while Taoists portray it as spillage. Our life power, basically, spills out of us. The entire target of contemplation and the catalytic practices in the East is to stop this spillage.

The wellspring of this spillage is in the psyche: irregular musings and negative feelings like displeasure, dread, and blame. (Blame squares the sacral chakra.)

In Tibetan Buddhism, they clarify that the wellspring of human enduring is the Three Poisons: fascination, revulsion, and daydream, or want, hostility, and obliviousness. Every one of the three harms cause spillage.

The Art of Seminal Retention (For Men Only)

A note for ladies: while this short area is about discharge in men, the data introduced here is still exceptionally pertinent to any lady who's right now in a relationship with a man or plans to have one.

A basic part of sexual change instructed in numerous antiquated ways of thinking from Asia and India is fundamental maintenance.

Original maintenance is the act of keeping away from discharge. These antiquated conventions accepted that they could develop their life power through fundamental maintenance to accomplish more noteworthy essentialness and life span.

Both the supplements inside the semen just as the life embodiment with the sperm itself, when held, can be utilized and consumed once again into your body to help your higher energy habitats, your sensory system, and your cerebrum. Have you ever seen a quick decrease in energy in the wake of discharging? Maybe you've noticed a slight feeling of gloom also?

The French expression La unimposing mort means "the little passing" and is utilized to depict a sexual climax. Imagine a scenario where men weren't intended to deliver their seed (aside from reproduction.

I'm not proposing this is fundamentally thus, yet it's an inquiry deserving of thought, for it is valid, it may help clarify the current helpless condition of manliness in our general public.

Meeting an Ancient Taoist

A couple of years back, I had the occasion to meet a man from China who professed to be 93 years of age. I state "professed to be" because he seemed as though he was in his mid-50s, and I was (and still am) somewhat wary.

In any case, he prepared in the antiquated Taoist ways. What's more, both of my qigong teachers who met with him were dazzled with his degree of aptitude, capacity, and information. (Both of these specialists have each prepared for more than 40 and 30 years, individually.)

This Taoist disclosed to me that in the old method of rehearsing these expressions, you avoid sex for the duration of your life—you never "break the seal," as it's been said in certain Taoist writings. He said that even Taoist nuns (ladies practice and train independently from men) swear off sex. At last, he said that this was the key to life span and developing one's energy.

As it says in the Hui-Ming Ching:

"When life energy isn't energized or mixed by want, we will get unfading."

Once more, I share this story only as a plan to ponder.

Discharge Frequency for Optimal Health

All things considered, in numerous Taoist writings, you'll discover rules for the recurrence of discharge that is alright for men keen on saving their life power.

The more youthful you are, the more life compels you have. As you get more established, this life power drains.

Youngsters: Sex once per day

- In your 20s: Once at regular intervals

- In your 30s: Once per week

- In your 40s: Once at regular intervals

- In your 60s: Once at regular intervals

Indications of over the top discharge incorporate constant weariness, stiffness in the joints, and agony in your knees and lower back.

Also, for sexual energy change, these recurrence ranges are presumably excessively liberal.

Shouldn't something be said about Pornography?

You won't discover much about sexual entertainment in old writings. Pornography is another difficulty that torment the most recent ages. Here, nonetheless, we can go to scientific exploration.

Studies show that sexual entertainment reworks the cerebrum, making it less associated and less dynamic.

Pornography use effectively gets habitual and addictive.

Masturbation and erotic entertainment make issues with excitement, sexual longing, and sexual execution.

Innumerable different examinations highlight the hurtful impacts of sexual entertainment. Here are some stunning details about pornography utilization.

From the setting of sexual change, erotic entertainment is maybe it's the best destroyer of sexual energy in men. If you need help with this region, look at the NoFap site or simply Google "nofap."

The Three Treasures of Taoism

For the rest of this sexual change management, I will take a more Eastern point of view.

Anybody acquainted with Taoism will know the three fortunes: Jing, Qi, and Shen.

Jing, Qi, and Shen are enthusiastic substances or frequencies that control numerous parts of our wellbeing, conduct, mind, and profound turn of events.

Be that as it may, despite the fact that these three fortunes are viewed as three different substances, they are of a similar embodiment, like how water can appear as gas, fluid, and strong (ice).

Jing – Essence

Jing is the most minimal vibration of the three fortunes. Numerous individuals botch Jing as sexual energy or original liquid, however, unnecessary sex drains one's Jing. Jing most intently makes an interpretation of in English to Life's Essence.

Qi – Energy

The Essence of the body converts to Qi (or Chi), which most intently means energy. Qi is a higher vibration than Jing, and it transports data all through the body's energy framework.

Shen – Spirit

Shen, the most elevated or most refined vibration, is the energy of cognizance. Numerous schools of Taoism consider Shen the person's

Spirit. Shen manifests as splendid white light, and its recurrence is nearest to Heaven.

Taoist Energy Transmutation: The Return of the Spirit

Seeing sexual change through the perspective of Taoism then, the essential objective in this cycle isn't material yet otherworldly.

The first chemists weren't early Western physicists endeavoring to change lead into gold. All things being equal, these antiquated Chinese Taoists were changing over the natural substances in their bodies.

These Inner Alchemists tried to refine their Jing into Qi by saving their Jing (through fundamental maintenance) and developing their Qi through a solid, adjusted lifestyle, virtuosity, and different Qigong works (counting standing contemplations like Zhan Zhuang).

Then, they tried to change over their Qi into Shen through thoughtful strategies intended to transform the body's middle into a cauldron that refines the Qi. This catalytic cycle changes their energy into Shen or the Original Spirit.

I'll give assets beneath to the individuals who are keen on investigating this point all the more profoundly.

Renew Your Jing with a Digital App?

OK, so what I will impart to you presently may seem like sci-fi.

Eric Thompson is an innovator and previous prime supporter of iAwake Technologies. A couple of years prior, Eric began Subtle Energy Sciences.

Utilizing quantum reverberation innovation, Eric designed a strategy for encoding advanced pictures with specific energy marks.

The outcome is the thing that he calls Digital Mandalas, which joins beautiful advanced workmanship with layers of different energy-related sound innovation.

If you're available to investigating new innovations as a guide to supporting your self-improvement, look at Eric's ongoing delivery called Audio Rejuvenation—a mix of advanced mandalas and soundtracks specifically intended to help renew your basic quintessence.

I generally have at any rate one advanced mandala running on my work area and my different gadgets.

Presently, if you don't have enthusiastic affectability, you may feel nothing from the start. If that is the situation, Eric offers different approaches to expand and improve the impacts.

Sexual Transmutation Starts with Healthy Kidneys

In Traditional Chinese Medicine, the kidneys are answerable for development, multiplication, urinary capacity, bones, cerebrum, and the storage facility of our pith (Jing).

If the kidneys are inadequate in what's called imperative qi, the watchman qi (the inconspicuous energy field around the body) will likewise be frail. Also, this inadequacy brings down the resistant framework, which influences the remainder of the body.

The kidneys are one of the basic organs in the human body, and we will generally give them little consideration.

Ill-advised guideline of sexual energy drains Jing and causes shortcoming in this organ over the long haul. Briskness in the appendages is a typical indication of kidney insufficiency.

Despite your explanation behind seeking after sexual change, it's a good thought to mend and strengthen your kidneys first.

Tips on How to Strengthen the Kidneys

There are numerous approaches to strengthen your kidneys and develop your Life Essence (sexual energy):

- Do a kidney purge.

- You can discover a ton of assets for kidney purges on the web. Hulda Clark's is maybe the most extensive.

- For my last kidney scrub, I utilized Renaltrex Kidney Cleanse from Global Healing Center.

- Eat an eating regimen that underpins kidney wellbeing.

Nourishments that help legitimate kidney work incorporate dark beans, kidney beans, blueberries, blackberries, spirulina, kelp, ocean growth, pumpkin seeds, dark sesame seeds, pecans, chestnuts, grain, millet, and dim, verdant green vegetables.

Attempt Chinese spices.

Take Six Flavor Teapills (Liu Wei Di Huang Wan) to help kidney wellbeing.

Maintain a strategic distance from cold nourishments and unreasonable crude food.

The kidneys and the liver don't care for anything cold—particularly during cold weather months and in chilly atmospheres. The more touchy you become to your body's energy framework, the loather to cold nourishments (like frozen yogurt) you'll probably turn into.

Lessen Your Media Utilization or Go on a 30-Day Media Quick

For what reason is this significant? Promoting, TV programming, computer games, and movies are dug in with sexual pictures intended to invigorate you. What's more, these pictures draw your energy out, if you need them as well. Numerous kinds of music like pop and R&B do as such as well.

Keep Away From Sexual Incitement For Half A Month

Dodge sexual movement, masturbation, or sexual incitement of any sort. In spite of the fact that Jing isn't sperm, men lose Jing through sex and discharge.

Monitoring your Essence is an essential key to sexual change.

Face Your Apprehensions

Every organ identifies with a specific prevalent feeling. For the kidneys, it's dread. Extreme dread harms the kidneys. Containing your dread is a fundamental advance for whole developed adulthood.

Practice Kidney Qigong

There are numerous practices in qigong that specifically focus on the kidneys. For instance, the seventh exercise in the Eight Brocades (Ba Daun Jin) and the kidney sound ("Chui") in the Six Healing Sounds.

The book Qigong Empowerment offers fantastic clinical qigong works out, including kidney qigong.

Avoid Your PDA and Innovation at All Costs

Over twelve investigations show that radiation from phones disable sperm work. Never keep your mobile phone in your jeans pockets, and consistently get it far from your head (consistently utilize a headset).

The Most Effective Method to Build a Foundation for Spiritual Energy

Changing sexual energy into profound energy can happen when the inward conditions are available. Also, it's dependent upon us to develop these inner conditions.

So what are these conditions?

Establishment #1: An Energetically Open Body

The body's enthusiastic framework must stream openly, however, for most people, we have numerous blockages all through the body. Qigong extending is intended to help tenderly open the body.

Then, figure out how to sink all your strain down into the ground through a training like Zhan Zhuang.

Establishment #2: A Calm, Abiding Mind

Considerations make strain in the body. When you're ready to calm your brain, your body's energy is normally saved.

There are numerous strategies for calming the psyche, including thoughtful works on breathing procedures and appropriate rest.

Establishment #3: A Lightened Mood

Dread, outrage, and reality all square the body's energy framework. Indeed, feelings stuck in the body are the essential wellspring of our vivacious blockage.

Helping one's brain opens lively channels. Access the bright kid in you and a feeling of fun loving nature.

Grin and murmur for reasons unknown by any stretch of the imagination. Have a go at getting a HeartMath emWave2 and practice their heart intelligence procedure.

Regardless of whether you didn't go any further, setting up these three establishments can fundamentally change your life experience to improve things.

CHAPTER 3. FEELINGS WITH PARTNER

Generally when you consider another age kind of way to deal with sexuality and getting it on, your vision naturally dreams with musings of insane yoga stances and reciting, and your noses flare, envisioning the incense and fragrant candles, all while an exploratory film is playing out of sight.

However, the thing about a careful way to deal with having intercourse, having climaxes, and commonly pleasuring yourself and your accomplice is that it doesn't need to feel totally in a strange spot or your typical daily practice.

Truth be told, when characterized in its easiest structure, tantric sex only intends to shape together different energies — which means those vibes you're giving and the ones your fortunate woman is shipping off your direction.

And keeping in mind that that doesn't really mean pheromones, tantric sex's advantages stretch out a long way past your cavort meetings and can really not just unite you as a team, yet lead you to a way of increased joy, satisfaction, and association with your everyday life.

Still not sold? Forget about it. Prepare to pick up all you require to think about tantric sex — directly from the specialists who have contemplated its old practices broadly.

Substance

If your sweetheart has convinced you to go to her week after a week yoga class (hi, dark tights, and descending canine!), then you've probably encountered some reciting and heard sanskrit. Despite the fact that not precisely the same thing, tantric sex has a rich history and advances thinking alongside that beating that you appreciate during intercourse, foreplay, and being a tease.

It's sort of a 'take a full breath and move slowly' way to deal with delight and keeping in mind that that may not generally be your flavor or speed, it can change the major way you perform sexually. "Tantra is a Sanskrit word in a real sense signifying 'loom, twist, weave.' The term 'Tantra,' after around 500 BCE, in Buddhism, Hinduism and Jainism is a bibliographic classification, much the same as the word Sutra (which signifies 'sewing together,' reflecting the representation of 'weaving together' inferred by Tantra).

With regards to sex wizardry, it carries together these components into the 'weaving together' of the sex accomplices," sex master and observer Coleen Singer says.

She adds: "It's a moderate type of sex that is said to expand closeness and make a brain-body association that can prompt amazing climaxes. It's additionally profoundly established in sex sorcery and otherworldliness and carries another profundity to couples rehearsing it. Tantric writings express that sexual activity can have three independent and unmistakable purposes: multiplication, joy, and freedom."

Tantric sex can likewise be called numerous things, contingent upon who you converse with or how you choose to rehearse. A portion of these cycles incorporate neotantra or navaratna, yet they all advance a similar thought:

The more in-order you are with your own body, yet the sensations you're feeling and the vibrations your accomplice is sending through her body, the better of an encounter it will be. Furthermore, — exposed with us here — yet some who practice tantra don't engage in sexual relations, however, are really abstinent, as they commend the life that comes from sex, rather than enjoying its obsessions.

Patricia Johnson and Mark Michaels, co-creators of Designer Relationships, Partners in Passion, Great Sex Made Simple, Tantra For Erotic Empowerment, and The Essence of Tantric Sexuality, note that characterizing tantra isn't a simple errand, since it's a different and profound custom. "

Tantra is an old Indian custom that perceives sexual energy as a wellspring of individual and otherworldly strengthening. It's imperative to comprehend that sexual energy could conceivably infer sexual movement.

The basic thought is that sexual energy is the life drive; it's what carried us into the world, and it's one of the most impressive inspirations in our lives," they clarify. "The more we can perceive and grasp this life power, the more completely human and engaged we will be."

One last approach to consider tantra is to consider the cognizance that comes when you completely grasp what your identity is, your cravings and the sparks around you, rather than stressing wholeheartedly over climaxing or how 'great' you are sleeping "Is anything but a procedure that makes your sexual encounters "Tantric," rather, it's a shift in demeanor, and this is accomplished by dragging out excitement and bringing as much mindfulness as possible to the movement," Johnson and Michael clarify.

Will I Enjoy Tantric Sex?

Notwithstanding an uplifting ability to be self-aware, a superior comprehension of your general surroundings, and permitting your sex life to develop past your bare bodies scouring together and really sharing a mind wave, tantric sex has more obvious down to earth purposes, as well. As a clinician, relationship apply, and creator of The Ultimate Guide to a Multi-Orgasmic Life, Antonia Hall, MA clarifies: Through Tantric sexual practices, one can figure out how to develop their inalienable sexual energy utilizing breath, muscle control and development of energy all through the body to take into consideration profoundly elevated delight. The two people can utilize the apparatuses of Tantric sex to become multi-orgasmic and have mind-twisting full-body climaxes."

By conversing with your accomplice about your longing to bring tantric sex into your wicked collection, you're showing a pledge to upgrading your sexual life to improve things.

While we'll discuss examining tantra later, Hall notes, "[Tantra] will change your sex life and take it higher than ever. Nothing is beyond reach in Tantra as long as the two individuals like the experiences. That opportunity, joined with the apparatuses of Tantra, will keep you appreciating multi-orgasmic ecstatic sex with your accomplice and open up totally different universes to you both."

Also, one final thing? Rehash after us — it's not insane, "new-age" or weird to need to evaluate tantra. "it's often seen as colorful and either excessively senseless or too exclusive to even consider being of interest or of incentive to common individuals.

This is awful because building up a Tantric way to deal with living can be helpful paying little heed to your conviction framework, and this methodology can be utilized in an assortment of settings, not simply in the room," Johnson and Michaels says.

The Most Effective Method to Talk To Your Partner About Tantric Sex

Ultimately and likely above all, opening up the exchange toward tantric practices is basic to making the experience commonly advantageous and life-evolving.

Having a discussion with your accomplice ought to never be tied in with being disappointed, but instead, you genuinely want to make your sex life all that it can (and should!) be for both of you. Likewise, with any discussion, approach it with an open heart and a benevolent tone.

"For some individuals, the hardest part is starting the discussion. So it's acceptable to start discussing sex as a rule. It's additionally imperative to have the option to communicate with each other all the manners in which you are content with your suggestive life together at this moment.

Very often, starting a discussion about sexual investigation can appear to be an analysis or send the message that you're not sexually fulfilled. It's critical to zero in on what's positive and move to the possibility of investigation from the point of view of plenitude not need.

'Things are so extraordinary, I was figuring it very well may be intriguing to investigate something new and extend our points of view, what's your opinion on that?'" Johnson and Michaels clarify.

When your accomplice is fascinated, consider disclosing to them how you trust tantric sex can be an excursion for both of you to partake in and something you take a shot at together to improve, energizing and well, fun.

Have you ever needed to back things off in the room and increase a more cozy association with an accomplice? If along these lines, you might need to think about tantric sex — a type of closeness zeroed in on strengthening the ties among you and your accomplice.

Here's the means by which to rehearse tantric sex and tips to incorporate the training into your sex life.

Tantric sex is a hindered adaptation of sex intended to upgrade closeness. It originates from the Sanskrit word tantra, which means woven together, and is established in Hindu and Buddhist lessons.

In tantric sex, the objective isn't tied in with arriving at climax rapidly (if by any stretch of the imagination) or about inclination mind-boggling actual joy. All things considered, tantric sex centers around making a certified careful association inside yourself and afterward among you and your accomplice.

"You feel as though you're consolidating or, rather, that the things that different you are hallucinations of the material world," says Stefani Goerlich, an authorized expert social specialist, and sex advisor. "The aftereffect of tantric practice is the formation of close securities with one's accomplice, more prominent attention to one's body, and the advancement of abilities, for example, care, limitation, and correspondence."

Step-by-Step Instructions to Quiet Nervousness

Another advantage of tantric sex is its capacity to ease uneasiness. Generally, closeness can cause execution nervousness around untimely discharge, erectile brokenness, and the stress over guaranteeing climax.

"That pressure... takes you from being at the time and in your body, to being in your mind," says Kamil Lewis, a sex and relationship specialist in Southern California.

Tantric sex eliminates those tensions. "When [you] can divert [your] center towards encountering the vibes of essentially being available and associated together, [you] can appreciate sex without nervousness or dread," says Goerlich.

Instructions to Get Ready for Tantric Sex

1. Find Out About Its Set of Experiences

Similarly as with any training established in a specific culture, setting aside the effort to comprehend its set of experiences shows regard for its root and permits you to grasp it with a more full agreement.

"We can't take on the otherworldly and strict acts of different societies without setting aside the effort to respect the sources and comprehend what we're doing," says Goerlich. An extraordinary spot to begin could be this social and chronicled review of tantra.

2. Practice Care

To plan for tantric sex, Lewis prescribes doing a care practice to interface with your body, gotten mindful of faculties, and delayed down — all fundamental parts of tantric sex.

3. Establish a Protected Climate

If attempting tantric sex, establish a protected climate where you and an accomplice don't hesitate to interface with yourselves and one another.

"Somewhere where you can feel uninhibited by interruptions, and someplace that you don't feel unsure about sounds you may make," says Lewis. "Groaning, snorting, and expressing are supported with tantric sex, so think about when flat mates, guardians, or kids aren't home."

Lewis likewise recommends joining quieting exotic components into space, for example, lit candles and basic oils.

Step-by-Step Instructions to Rehearse Tantric Sex

1. Zero in on Breath

Zeroing in on breath is a fundamental segment of tantric sex, as it takes into consideration a more profound association. Accomplices are urged to synchronize their breaths, so it nearly becomes one development, says Molly Papp, LMFT, sexologist, a certified sex habit advisor, and proprietor of Bella Vida Therapy.

The most effective method to rehearse careful breathing and the demonstrated advantages that it offers

Likewise, with most care rehearses, the breath additionally grounds you right now. Take a stab at focusing on a piece of your body where you feel the breath, similar to the stomach or chest, and pull together your thoughtfulness regarding this part.

2. Look into One Another's Eyes

Invest energy looking into an accomplice's eyes. While ceaseless eye to eye connection isn't important for tantric sex, Papp strongly prescribes it often happens to help fabricate a close association. Eye staring is another method of synchronizing one another's energy. To look further, give centering a shot having your correct eye interface with their correct eye.

3. Slow Down

Tantric sex isn't a rush to an orgasmic finish line, yet an opportunity to back off and investigate each other's bodies. It can go on until you arrive at climax, feel associated, or are genuinely fulfilled.

This disposition change eases a great deal of regularly felt nervousness. "It is particularly incredible for ladies because of its emphasis on easing back things down and trusting that excitement will construct," says Papp. "

During a time where we are overwhelmed with ridiculous strain to feel orgasmic joy in no time, this is liberating for some ladies."

Papp recommends having lube, oils, or salve close by to guarantee sluggish developments aren't agonizing.

4. Connect Each of the Five Detects

The main "objective" of tantric sex is staying present and monitoring sensations in the body. To do this, Lewis proposes focusing on every one of the five of your faculties, not simply contact.

"Notice how your accomplice smells, what the bends of their bodies resemble, what tastes you get in your mouth as you kiss, what it seems like when they or you groan," Lewis says. "These are on the whole extraordinary approaches to get grounded in your body and present at the time."

5. Fuse Rub

Sex shouldn't be penetrative. "Kissing, contacting, holding, scouring, and more would all be able to prompt a full tantric sexual experience, no infiltration vital," says Lewis.

Regardless of whether you need to join penetrative sex, Goerlich says there's no motivation to race into it. Start by zeroing in on markers that keep you present and associated, such as kneading or nestling.

"Delay this tangible investigation and convey it over into your penetrative sex — if without a doubt you have penetrative sex," says Goerlich.

Truth be told, zeroing in on different types of closeness can help keep tension levels down.

"Something more erotic instead of sexual could help quiet one or the two accomplices," says Papp. "A nestle meeting or back rub would help soothe that tension and facilitate the experience."

Tantric sex hinders a personal encounter and stresses the association between you and an accomplice.

The training includes zeroing in on the breath, remaining present, and establishing a protected climate to investigate arousing closeness.

It's a lot simpler to share your contemplations, the scholarly data that is in your mind, than your emotions. Sharing the profundity of your sentiments that are in your heart faces an enthusiastic challenge and mental fortitude.

This causes you to feel uncovered and powerless, yet it is the very thing that will make closeness and association in your marriage. By sharing what is in your heart with your mate, you can accomplish further intimacy.

Instructions to Share Your Feelings With Your Spouse

Attempt these tips to assist you with feeling more good and set up to impart to your life partner.

Acknowledge that emotions are neither right nor wrong. The conduct results because of the inclination that is ethically judged. Because you are furious doesn't give you the option to be fierce. Negative emotions actually should be managed properly.

Depict the inclination by saying it or composing it. One objective is to enable your accomplice to comprehend what it resembles to stroll from your perspective. You probably need compassion and comprehension as a trade-off for sharing your sentiments.

Name the inclination. Utilize a rundown of feeling words if this is difficult. Recall that emotions are a single word: miserable, furious, hurt, upbeat, excited, humiliated, etc.

Practice. If you are not somebody who is accustomed to communicating emotions, this may feel off-kilter from the outset. Rehearsing it in little advances will make it simpler.

Understand that emotions go back and forth and change rapidly. This is different from a "temperament" which is a continued time of an enthusiastic state.

Perceive considerations versus emotions. Thinking, otherwise called "cognizance" is a cycle that happens in our minds. It flocks our contemplations and convictions about something. Sentiments, then again, pass on our passionate state and is often said to come from the heart. Sentiments can likewise be actual sensations.

Offer your more profound fundamental inclination, not simply surface sentiments.

You may be communicating outrage, yet underneath, feel hurt or humiliated. This is significantly more vital to communicate to your accomplice to create closeness and closeness.

Attempt to not judge your or your companion's emotions. If you need your life partner to keep on sharing on this level, it is significant not to get bothered or guarded about the inclination communicated to you.

Utilize the 'I think versus I feel' rule. If you can substitute the words 'I think' for 'I feel' in a sentence, then you have communicated thought and not an inclination.

For instance, "I feel hurt" is right because you would not say, "I think hurt,' correct? Somebody may state, "I feel that he is a snap" is inaccurate. You "think" he is a snap.

Express emotions with your life partner straightforwardly. Your life partner can't guess what you might be thinking. The individual in question may get on your vibe, yet they have no real way to realize what is in your mind, except if you reveal it!

Different Details to Remember

Offer your sentiments with one another day by day. You don't must have profound, genuine discussions about your relationship day by day, however, you do need to share your sentiments (not simply your contemplations) about what is new with you every day. It's significant not to settle on choices dependent on emotions.

When dynamic, emotions will be a piece of the cycle, yet you should think intelligently and objectively.

Saying that you were "late for a gathering" gives the fundamental data as it were. Be that as it may, saying you "felt humiliated about being late for a gathering" encourages you to associate with the individual you are talking with. In like manner, dismissing an inclination is dismissing the individual inclination.

Try not to make statements like "Don't stress, be glad" or "You shouldn't feel that way." Doing so nullifies how the other individual feels.

To be effective at sharing your sentiments, you should be open, genuine, ready to set aside a few minutes for one another, and responsive to these talks.2 This should be a corresponding cycle. You both must share on a cozy level with one another. It can't simply be one of you.

Realizing how to communicate your sentiments is vital to having a genuinely satisfying relationship. Opening up and being helpless makes closeness. However, being able to share your sentiments goes past saying, "I love you." Good correspondence likewise implies having the option to communicate when you're feeling feelings that are awkward, like bitterness, disillusionment, or outrage. Having the option to impart your sentiments to your accomplice is something that doesn't come effectively to everybody. Yet, with some time and a little work, it is possible for anybody.

CHAPTER 4. PLEASURE VIBRATORS

Vibrators are the most mainstream of all sex toys available, and it's no big surprise: When something vibrates against the sensitive privates or inside the vagina or anus, all the sensitive spots wake up. To place it in plain terms: Vibrators feel great. They can get you in the mind-set, turn you on, warm you up, make you hot, and get you off. I can't reveal to you the number of stories I've gotten with ladies who encountered their absolute first climax by utilizing a vibrator. Truly when we start to stroke off, we're aren't specialists immediately, and a few ladies find that they can't get the specific procedure down to carry themselves to climax.

At the point when they attempt a vibrator, it conveys predictable, centered stimulation that may assist them with accomplishing what was once subtle. Numerous ladies use vibrators during masturbation to become more acquainted with their bodies better, find what sorts of stimulation they like, and afterward give that data to their partners. And keeping in mind that it might appear as though vibrators are only for ladies, they aren't! A lot of men appreciate utilizing vibrating sleeves or siphons and conventional vibrators to animate the top of their penis, their balls, or their perineum. A portion of the more gutsy ones use vibrators for anal stimulation.

Vibrators aren't only for solo investigation it is possible that; they're superb for collaborated sex. Consider a vibrator your "additional arrangement of hands" in the room: While you're doing a certain something, it very well may be doing another. Is it true that one is hand working her areolas and the other one stroking her hair? A vibrator can be scouring her vulva when you have your hands full. Need to zest up oral sex for him? While you have one hand on his shaft and your lips folded over him, slip a vibrator facing his balls. Can't reach to animate her clitoris during intercourse in a specific position? Vibrator to the salvage!

For certain ladies, a vibrator can be a major assistance in getting them stirred. Do you have a low drive? Provided that this is true, it can take you a long effort to get turned on, and you can get disappointed by the cycle; intellectually and inwardly, your craving is super hot, however your body can't get up to speed. A vibrator can resemble an easy route: It assists with getting you loose, turned on, and greased up faster.

Exploration shows that most of ladies need clitoral stimulation to have a climax; it very well may be clitoral stimulation all alone or joined with penetration, however the clit should be in the blend! Also, we're not discussing any old sort of stimulation. There are a lot of partners who can utilize their fingers, mouths, tongues or some mix to bring a lady joy, yet numerous ladies need delayed, directed stimulation on their clitoris to climax. Let's be honest: People can run out of steam. Their jaws get sore, their necks start to squeeze, and their fingers begin to back off—yet a vibrator simply continues going! Furthermore, a vibrator can convey a sort of stimulation no human can, stimulation that is predictable and ground-breaking—the ideal mix of speed, pressure, movement, power, and musicality.

Choose a Viberator That Works for You

There is a particularly wide assortment of vibrators available that perusing at your neighborhood sex shop or online can once in a while be overpowering. The best spot to begin is to choose what you'd like your vibrator to do. Do you need it for outside clitoral stimulation just, penetration, or one that can do both? Shouldn't something be said about a vibrato that is intended for synchronous penetration and clitoral stimulation? Whenever you've chosen about its capacity, at that point you can proceed onward to what you need it to resemble. There are insertable vibrators made to look as near a human penis as could be expected under the circumstances, with various skin tones, veins, circumcised heads, and in some cases balls. There are others that have a reasonable penis-like shape, yet come in lively shadings like pink, red, green, or purple. Others are intended to take after something natural like a container of lipstick or an adorable creature. Some are totally harmless looking: little, prudent devices a great many people wouldn't take a second look at. A few vibrators resemble show-stoppers, with smooth current shapes, first in class materials, and glossy silk lined cases.

You ought to consider all the components examined in part 3, including size, cost, and brand and audit the various materials shrouded in section

4. Most vibrators are made of elastic, PVC, elastomer, TPR, hard plastic, silicone, or some blend. Moreover, vibrators are mechanized, so they have some particular highlights to consider. To start with, what's your speed? A few vibrators have one speed (it's on or it's off); others have a decision of a few paces. Some have dials that let you continuously speed up, and others have a reach from delicate to take your breath away. When in doubt, battery-fueled vibrators have less extraordinary vibration than their module partners, and the more batteries, the more grounded the force. Electric vibrators are considered at the highest point of the load for their capacity, yet you need to have a source close by to utilize them!

Notwithstanding the force and speed of the vibration, numerous vibrators offer various kinds of vibration. For instance, Vibrators like the Form 6 by Jimmyjane and the SaSi offer various modes, which range moving from shuddering to undulating to plying—every one of which delivers an alternate sensation. These are the up and coming age of vibrators that go past a one- size-fits-all model and endeavor to give you a redid experience.

You may likewise have to consider how boisterous a vibrator is, on the grounds that they range from the silent kind to the sort that seems like a little machine running. On the off chance that you have flat mates, slim dividers, meddling neighbors, or youngsters, you might need to pick a vibrator on the calmer finish of the range. At last, not all vibrators are waterproof. Those that are will obviously express this component on the bundle or in the depiction; waterproof vibrators are anything but difficult to clean (since they can be lowered in water) and are incredible for individuals who like to play in the shower, shower, hot tub, or pool.

To give you a superior feeling of what's accessible, in the following six sections, we'll survey the various types of vibrators, alongside their highlights, how to utilize them, and a few hints for joining them into solo and banded together sex. They include:

• Compact clitoral vibrators: little, watchful, battery-fueled or battery-powered, intended for outside clitoral stimulation, low to direct vibration; useful for apprentices, simple to go with

• Plug-in clitoral vibrators: bigger, module, intended for outer clitoral stimulation, moderate to extraordinary vibration; unparalleled force for the individuals who need solid vibration

• Wearable and sans hands vibrators: exceptional shapes that you can lash on, sit on, or slip inside during intercourse

• Insertable vibrators: phallic and bended, battery-controlled or battery-powered, intended for penetration and G-spot stimulation

• Dual-activity vibrators: battery-controlled or battery-powered, intended for concurrent penetration and clitoral stimulation; this gathering incorporates "bunny" Vibrators

• Smart vibrators: up and coming age of toys that component cutting edge innovation, fluctuated highlights, and top-quality plan and materials

• Vibrating cock rings, sleeves, and siphons for men will be highlighted in later sections.

Tips for Buying Your First Vibrator

Like other "firsts," purchasing your first vibrator is serious! Finding out pretty much all the various types of vibrators is a decent advance toward finding what's out there. Next, attempt to accumulate data and counsel from some genuine individuals. You can get some information about their inclinations, visit a quality sex shop with learned sales reps, go to an in-home sex toy gathering, or read client surveys of items on sex toy sites. Search for a vibrator with numerous paces, so you can have choices. I prescribe picking one with low to direct vibration to begin. In the event that you discover you need more force, you can generally overhaul. However, on the off chance that you begin with something as incredible as the Hitachi Magic Wand, it might basically be excessively extraordinary and may turn you off of the vibrator experience. It's ideal to choose something reasonable in the event that you don't wind up cherishing it. Save the costly extravagance vibrators for when you're certain about what you like.

Using a Clitoral Vibrator

They may accompany batteries or a jazzy conveying case, however most vibrators don't accompany guidelines! You'll discover explicit tips in ensuing sections about utilizing various kinds of vibrators, however we should begin for certain fundamentals that apply to every single clitoral vibrator. Before you turn it on, you might need to warm yourself up with your own hand or a partner's hand or mouth. Truth be told, a few ladies like bunches of foreplay before a vibrator enters the image at all since they require to be truly excited. In the event that they aren't heated up, the stimulation feels excessively serious and doesn't feel pleasurable. A few people like to have bunches of play, including some intercourse, prior to going after their favorite vibrator. For other people, the vibrator is a surefire technique to heat up—it's the way to lighting their sensual fire.

Whatever your inclination, consistently start on a moderate speed from the outset. Make certain to touch some grease as an afterthought that interacts with your body. Start by putting the vibrator against your internal and external labia and your vaginal opening. Maintain a strategic distance from the clitoris from the start as you allow your body to fire up. Steadily speed up on the off chance that you need to (and if that is an alternative). At the point when you're prepared, move it aside of your clitoral hood. You need to move toward the clitoris by implication initially to allow yourself to become acclimated to the stimulation. Attempt each side of the hood, at that point attempt the vibrator straightforwardly on top of the hood—the hood, not simply the glans. Most ladies find that a vibrator on top of or aside of the clitoral hood is bounty invigorating; notwithstanding, a few ladies like it when you really pull back the clitoral hood and uncover the clitoral glans for direct stimulation. A few ladies like to do this periodically or just when they are extremely, turned on. Attempt it and perceive how it feels for you, and make certain to tell your partner your inclination. On the off chance that you discover the slowest speed of your vibrator excessively extraordinary in any event, for circuitous stimulation, here are a couple of stunts to diminish the force:

• Keep your clothing on while you utilize the vibrator, so the texture will somewhat quiet the vibration.

• Put a washcloth between your vulva and the vibrator; overlay it more than once relying upon the amount you need to diminish the power.

• Place your fingers or hand (or those of your partner) among you and the vibrator; this can diffuse the vibration.

Whenever you've become accustomed to it, you can explore different avenues regarding various paces, changing measures of pressing factor, and distinctive vibration modes if your vibrator has them. A few people like to move the vibe against them, while others like to keep it still and let the vibration itself be the lone movement. Regardless of whether you are separated from everyone else or with an partner, investigate various situations to locate the best ones for you.

CHAPTER 5. SEX TOYS FOR HIM

Penis Sleeves and Pumps

Penis sleeves and siphons are among the most mainstream masturbation toys for men. Much the same as for ladies, masturbation is a significant piece of a man's sexual coexistence. It's a possibility for him to interface with his body, investigate his sexual longings and dreams, attempt new things, and improve familiar with his preferences. Masturbation isn't only for single men or men who are away from their partners! Notwithstanding your sexual movement, all men should remove time from their bustling lives to stroke off, and penis sleeves and siphons are an extraordinary method to encounter new sensations or zest up your self-joy schedule. On the off chance that you need to figure out how to draw out intercourse, utilizing a penis sleeve is an extraordinary method to rehearse how to control and defer discharge. A few men use penis siphons for masturbation, yet to assist them with accomplishing an erection or get a more grounded one.

Sleeves are made of jam elastic, PVC, elastomer, warm plastics (with reserved names like CyberSkin and Real Feel Super Skin), or silicone and arrive in an assortment of styles. Most sleeves have some sort of surface within, both to invigorate sensitive pieces of the penis and to reenact intercourse. A few sleeves have a straightforward, rounded plan with an opening at the two finishes, while others have openings intended to resemble a mouth, a vagina, or a butt. A few sleeves are shaped from the private parts of porno stars.

Sleeves come in one size and will in general be very stretchy to oblige various estimated penises. In case you're searching for a particularly cozy fit, a few organizations make "extra close" renditions. All sleeves include a finished inside with stubs, knocks, edges, rings, or knobs. Some are shaped to feel like the dividers of a vagina. Some have edges or tight rings at the opening to mimic the kickoff of a vagina or a butt. Some penis sleeves can be reasonable, yet purchaser be careful: Those made of mediocre materials and development can tear effectively, delivering the toy pointless. Do your examination, read toy audits on sites, and approach a sales rep for a proposal.

Prior to utilizing a sleeve, put it into a bowl of extremely warm or heated water. This will warm the toy and cause it to feel more like skin. Shake the overabundance water out, at that point empty your favorite lube into the opening and coat your penis with lube too. (Recall never to utilize silicone lubes with silicone or warm plastic sleeves.) Lube is a significant part for sleeves to function admirably. The thought is clear: You slide your penis into the sleeve, and the material holds it snuggly. As you move the sleeve all over, the surface and snugness of the sleeve invigorates the penis, a sensation like having sex. You can likewise keep the sleeve still and move all through the sleeve; this procedure works best with a sleeve like the Fleshlight, which is housed in a hard case. You can likewise wedge a sleeve between the bedding and box spring of your bed for without hands pushing; this works best if the tallness of your bed permits you to stand or bow serenely when you do it. A few sleeves have vibrators appended to them for additional stimulation; you can likewise utilize any vibrator toward the finish of a sleeve.

Despite the fact that they are more hard to track down, there are likewise penis sleeves that are intended for a man to slip over his penis and wear during intercourse. The sleeve adds both length and size to his penis, has a surface to invigorate his partner's vagina, and regularly vibrates. Truly outstanding in this class is the Vibrating O Sleeve accessible at Babeland.

To keep a sleeve's surface and make it last, it's essential to perfect and dry the sleeve altogether just after you use it. A few sleeves can be cleaned with mellow cleanser and water or a sex toy cleaner, while others must be cleaned with water. Adhere to guidelines on the bundle.

The Fleshlight

The Fleshlight is the top penis sleeve available, a novel item that earns rave surveys from men all over. A person once disclosed to me that utilizing a Fleshlight was superior to sex with a condom, it felt that extraordinary! In contrast to different sleeves, this sleeve sits in a plastic packaging (which resembles a monster electric lamp, henceforth the name). Since it's for a situation, it makes an astounding attractions sensation. Furthermore, you can turn the cap on the finish to increment or lessening the measure of pull. You can likewise eliminate the cap out and out and stick a little vibrator in the opening on the finish to vibrate against the top of the penis. It's made of a protected without phthalate plastic considered Real Feel Super Skin that has an incredibly sensible fleshlike surface.

You can eliminate the sleeve itself for cleaning, and the maker suggests that you just clean it with warm water (no cleanser), shake out the overabundance water, and let it dry. After it dries, you should tidy it with cornstarch—just cornstarch, never infant powder or powder. This encourages it keep up its one of a kind surface. In the event that you don't clean it, it will turn out to be incredibly tacky and crude and difficult to utilize.

Penis Pumps Will Make Him Harder

Penis siphons have a chamber and a pneumatic machine; when you make a vacuum seal, you power freshen up of the chamber with the siphon. That brings blood into the penis, starting the engorgement cycle and giving a man an erection. Men use penis siphons for an assortment of reasons: they appreciate the pull sensation; to assist them with getting an erection; to assist them with getting a more grounded erection; or to get an erection that keeps going longer. Notwithstanding some advertising claims, penis siphons can't and won't make your penis greater. A few men do say that after long haul use, the shaft of the penis is better characterized (similarly as different muscles in the body become all the more very much characterized in the wake of working out). On the off chance that you have diabetes, circulatory issues, specific kinds of erectile brokenness, malignant growth, or another genuine ailment, counsel a doctor prior to utilizing a penis siphon.

There are basically two various types of siphons, which I call the fundamental siphon and the high level siphon; the chambers in either kind are made of plastic or slim acrylic. A fundamental siphon is a chamber associated with a cylinder with a delicate oval-molded hand-crush siphon on the end. Fundamental siphons will in general be more affordable than cutting edge siphons, and they're a decent spot to begin on the off chance that you've never purchased a siphon and are uncertain about whether you'll like it. These siphons ordinarily have an opening on top or the side that you need to cover while you siphon and reveal to deliver the pressing factor once you have an erection. A high level siphon has a chamber associated with tubing that is associated with a single handed grip siphon; the siphon has a pressing factor measure on it and a fast delivery tab. Some state these are more secure in light of the fact that you can perceive the amount you are siphoning on the check; you can likewise take note of the specific number on the measure to recall for sometime later. The speedy delivery tab implies it is more advantageous on the grounds that you don't need to hold your finger or hand over an opening, since your hand can sneak through the cycle.

Some penis siphons have vibrators appended to them for additional stimulation during the siphoning cycle. Some have connections you can put on the initial that are made of a gentler material, (for example, jam elastic, silicone, or warm plastic); the delicate connection lounges around the base of your penis and makes it more agreeable and pleasurable for a few, sort of like joining a penis sleeve and a siphon into one toy.

To utilize a penis siphon, rub lube around the erupted opening of the chamber and on the base of your penis; the thought is to make a vacuum seal. In case you're experiencing difficulty making a tight seal, you may require more lube or you may have to manage or shave your pubic hair. Put the chamber over your penis. In the event that there is an opening in the top or on one side, cover it with your finger or hand. With the hand siphon, give it a couple of siphons and perceive how it feels. On the off chance that you have additional skin or the skin of your scrotal sac is free, it can get sucked into the chamber, which a few people like. On the off chance that you need to evade that, hold your sac away from the chamber as you siphon. Go gradually and never siphon to the point that it harms. You ought to likewise never siphon for over 15 minutes. When you have an erection, quit siphoning and leave the chamber on for a couple of moments; this will proceed with the engorgement cycle. Delivery the air from the chamber by eliminating your hand from the opening or utilizing a speedy delivery valve, if the siphon has one.

Siphoning while in the shower or shower is fun, on the grounds that the genital tissue is warm and can grow simpler, yet ensure you have a waterproof, shower safe siphon. You can likewise siphon just after a hot shower or shower. A few men like to put on a rooster ring in the wake of siphoning to keep up the impacts; you can peruse more about cock rings in the following part.

The Hugger

The Hugger is a vibrator planned particularly for penis stimulation. It's fundamentally a slug formed vibrator with a cup connection that looks like a topsy turvy tulip. The cup embraces the head, and the petals vibrate against it, conveying vibration to the most sensitive piece of the penis.

CONCLUSION

There's no rulebook, per state, yet at the core of tantra are sexual customs that get you in the temperament and assist you with interfacing with your accomplice. One big deal: "loving" or serving one another.

Accomplices turn the attention on each other (like through back rub), which delays and constructs excitement, state Patricia Johnson and Mark Michaels, co-creators of Tantra for Erotic Empowerment and The Essence of Tantric Sexuality.

Maybe the best piece of tantric sex is that it benefits everybody. "Tantra can help men experiencing untimely discharge because it hinders the cycle of sex and eliminates the strain to perform," says Tammy Nelson, Ph.D. authorized psychotherapist, relationship master, and creator of Getting the Sex You Want. "For ladies, figuring out how to unwind and be at the time can help with orgasmic work just as building want."

It can likewise help your relationship outside the room by improving close correspondence.

While climaxes aren't the objective, per state, "tantric climaxes" are often alluded to as supernatural encounters, says Sally Valentine, Ph.D., a certified sex specialist in Boca Raton, Florida.

Sign me up, isn't that so? Be that as it may, how the hell do you take the plunge? To begin with, talk it over with your accomplice. Give them the deets on what it is and why you need to attempt it (you know: further closeness, energy, additionally fulfilling sex, or for no particular reason). When your boo offers the go-ahead, begin joining the specialty of tantra into your sex routine with these straightforward advances.

Get into the temperament is by joining ceremonies into sex. That can be anything, for example, setting up your space as an asylum with candles, pads, and delicate music.

What's most significant is that you cause sex to feel, well, uncommon. "You need a feeling that sex is something significant and particular from regular day to day existence," state Johnson and Michaels.

"Sutra" in Sanskrit implies composition; "Kama" alludes to want, delight or sex. Hence: Treatise on Desire/Pleasure/Sex. For Vatsyayana, nonetheless, want/delight/sex holds a different importance than for us worldweary moderns excessively acquainted with commoditized sex.

Want, joy and sex in the Kama Sutra are contextualized, seen as a feature of a perspective where people move together in expressions of the human experience of affection and in families and in bigger organizations of relations.

Similarly likewise with yoga, tantra starts with and bases on the breath. Attempt this technique suggested by Valentine: Take a full breath in through your nose. On the breathe in, top off your midsection with air.

Breathe out. (It is safe to say that you are doing it, right? When you place your hands over your stomach, you should feel it develop the breath in and profit to typical for the breath out.)

Picture that you're pushing the breath down through your pelvis, knees, and floor. Practice the midsection breathing strategy a few times before you bring it into sex with the goal that it turns out to be more programmed, she suggests.

Eye to eye connection will help both of you feel nearer during sex. Zero in on one another. Generally, this is by investigating their left eye, yet you can investigate both if that is more agreeable to you.

"Deferring climax often intensifies the experience," said Johnson and Michaels. "Staying in a high condition of excitement can likewise assist individuals with encountering vigorous climaxes, or climaxes without discharging," they add.

Deferring a climax implies you carry yourself to the bring of having one, just to chill out and postpone it. Called edging, it's ideal to try it out while stroking off to understand the method.

Work on getting yourself up to the point of climax, then halting, and firing up once more.

Then, when you're with your accomplice, you can alternate getting each other up toward the peak, sliding down, and afterward returning up again toward climax prior to giving up to the firecrackers finale.

Most importantly, take out this thought from your brain that it's not what acceptable young ladies do because numerous young ladies talk hot. Most men like such talk.

They likewise like young ladies who are prepared to assume responsibility in their grasp. Your better approach for talking and utilizing such conversation starters from the given models would excite him.

If you have not yet arrived at the sexual relationship, then utilize these lines which are not exceptionally 'dirty':

• I like your body

• When you touch me, I feel some electric flow through my body.

• You have a decent figure

If you get apprehensive before his essence and can't attempt these lines, then take a stab at utilizing them over a telephone:

• Your voice is turning me on

• What are you wearing (with enchanting voice)?

• Where is your hand?

• Can I rub your...

Here is the means by which to play out this sex procedure: Take any sex position and don't concentrate on just the entrance part of it. Or maybe when playing out any sex demonstration, screw with your penis!

As you penetrate your accomplice, screw with your penis clockwise. By screwing you are squeezing and invigorating the clitoris, which will conceivably prompt a dangerous female climax.